The
Stop
Junk
Mail
Book

by Dorcas S. Miller

Georgetown Press
Augusta, Maine

This book is dedicated to Ben,
my friend, sweetheart, and husband.

ISBN 0-9628753-0-9
First Edition
Printed in the United States of America

This book is printed on recycled paper.

For ordering information, contact:
Georgetown Press
RFD 2, Box 535
Augusta, Maine 04330
(207) 582-5600

Design & Graphics by Nina Medina, Somerville, Maine
Printed by Courier Companies

Do You Know That—

- In 1988, U.S. businesses and non-profit organizations mailed out over 63 billion pieces of third-class mail, averaging 84 pounds per household?
- A two percent response to a mail solicitation is a good response — the other 98 percent is simply a "cost of doing business"?
- From 10 to 50 percent of the price of a mail-order product goes toward paper, printing, postage, and name rental?
- Each year, your favorite charitable organization may be handing out your name and address to hundreds of other groups?
- If you ask, many mail-order companies and charities will *stop* giving your name away?

The Stop Junk Mail Book tells you how to reduce unsolicited mail sent to your home and outlines your options for returning mail to the sender or the Post Office. Most importantly, the book includes 32 postcards to help you accomplish these goals easily.

SHOE

Reprinted by permission: Tribune Media Services

Table of Contents

Acknowledgments

Thanks to the following people for providing assistance: Chet Dalzell, Direct Marketing Association; Bonnie Dahan and Ted Tuescher, Smith & Hawken; Judy Enck, New York Public Interest Research Group; Phil Girton, Seventh Generation; Michael Fenton, Goodman & Sons; Jackie Prince, Environmental Defense Fund; Bob Schaeffer, Conservatree Paper Company; Cynthia Strout, Freeport Recycling Center; Sharon Treat, Maine House of Representatives; Marie Weinmann, Natural Resources Defense Council; Mike West, U.S. Postal Service; and Ann Wilcox, Massachusetts Public Interest Research Group.

Thanks also to Evelyn de Frees, Rebecca Stanley, and Ben Townsend for providing valuable suggestions and encouragement.

Preface

For over six years I worked at the Natural Resources Council of Maine, a non-profit environmental organization. Our agenda was wide-ranging — recycling, air pollution, clean water, energy conservation, land use planning, and other important issues. One of our major victories during those years was a sweeping law that set some of the most aggressive state waste reduction and recycling goals in the nation.

As I worked as the Council, I looked more closely at what was in my own garbage bag and discovered that a big chunk of my garbage was unsolicited mail. I registered with Direct Marketing Association and cut my direct mail substantially. I wrote to organizations and asked that my name not be traded or sold. I sent cards to companies and charities which solicited me and asked to be taken off their mailing lists. And I realized that curtailing unsolicited mail was a full-time occupation.

Meanwhile, at the office, I published the address for the Direct Marketing Association in our newsletter; members wrote back saying, "Thanks!" I wrote several commentaries about junk mail for Maine's public radio sys-

...I realized that curtailing unsolicited mail was a full-time occupation.

Ms. Finchpink, Vice President
Curtailer of Unsolicited Mail

tem; listeners responded with their frustrations and successes.

I decided that the Council had to bring its office practices more in line with its environmental policies. We used direct mail to recruit new members, and I knew that many of our solicitations went straight into the waste basket and on to the landfill. There had to be a better way.

First, I proposed that the organization do smaller mailings to better targeted audiences. Second, I set up a "take me off your list" list, so that people who wished to do so could get off our mailing list for five years. Third, I designed and mailed to our members a set of eight postcards that they could use at home to help cut back on the amount of junk mail they received.

I was told that these cards would be a terrible mistake because our members could mail them back to us, requesting that their names not be traded to other organizations for future solicitation. If we had fewer names to barter, we would receive fewer names in return. We would hurt our efforts to get new members.

My response was that cutting down on the amount of waste that we produced was worth having fewer names to trade. We might even get more members, people who approved of our in-house efforts to solve environmental problems.

The reaction from members was immediate and hearty. "Your Junk Mail Attack Kit is fabulous! Thank you!" "This wonderfully named Junk Mail Attack Kit is the single best small-scale environmental idea I've recently seen." "Your junk mail postcards are wonderful! Send me more."

"Send me more." It was clear that eight cards were not enough for people being inundated by junk mail. After I left the Council, I continued to think about what would be "enough." Thirty cards, perhaps, with an explanation of direct mail and specific strategies for getting off mailing lists?

Thus, *The Stop Junk Mail Book* was born. With this book, you can deal with an aggravating problem — unsolicited first- and third-class mail — and help protect the environment. Regrettably, this book does not deal with the bulky advertising supplements that arrive, second class, with newspapers. So far, I have not discovered a way to curtail this material.

This book is not a condemnation of direct mail, which does have a place in our society. Direct mail can be a valid way for people to sell products and for organizations to state their cases. I am one of the 98.6 million people in the U.S. who order merchandise by mail. I do so because mail-order saves me time and gasoline. I also read the newsletters from non-profit organizations — sent bulk rate — to keep informed of their activities. Not all advertising or third-class mail is junk.

What *is* junk mail? For me, it's mail (other than bills) that I didn't ask for and don't want. It's the mail that goes straight into the trash without ever being opened. It's the mail that I don't read and can't recycle.

Here are the strategies and the cards. All you need to supply is a pen, a book of stamps, a roll of tape, and half an hour of your time.

Dorcas S. Miller

How Direct Mail Works

Any time you give your name and address, whether you're subscribing to a publication, registering to vote, getting your driver's license, placing a credit card order, entering a sweepstakes, ordering through the mail, joining an organization, or donating to charity, you are providing someone with the means to solicit you later.

Names are gold in the direct mail business, where lists are rented for $50 to $150 per 1,000 names. A magazine that rents 10,000 of its subscribers' names at 10 cents each can clear a tidy profit ($1,000 minus a broker's fee) without ever having to ask anyone for money. Business in list rental is brisk, involving $3 billion per year at last count. Although some organizations and businesses, like AT&T, Red Cross, and *Reader's Digest*, do not rent their lists, thousands of companies and charitable organizations do.

In direct mail, names are gold.

Most non-profit charities depend on "prospecting"—sending mailings to non-members to increase membership. Due to the high cost of renting names, non-profits will often trade their members' names with other non-profits. Their members reap the reward—a pile of unsolicited letters asking for donations. A small non-profit may trade half a dozen times a year, while large ones may trade 50 or more times annually. One national organization reported that its lists were sold or traded to "hundreds" of organizations per year.

Even a group with only 5,000 members may generate 150,000 pieces of junk mail annually in an effort to increase membership. Greenpeace USA reportedly mails more than 47 million pieces a year. According to the U.S. Postal Service, in 1988 non-profit organizations (including charities, churches, and educational institutions) mailed out over 11 billion pieces of third-class mail.

In the non-profit world, a mailing that breaks even is

considered a success, because the real profit is not from immediate donations or memberships, but the money that will be generated from those names in the future. For example, a mailing of 100,000 pieces at 53 cents each costs $53,000. A two percent response (considered successful in the industry) means donations from 2,000 people. If the average donation is $26.50, then the mailing breaks even.

But a person who donates once is more likely to donate again. When the organization does a follow-up mailing to those 2,000 people, if even half donate again at $26.50 each, there will be a net income of $25,440 ($26,500 minus the cost of mailing).

Of course, this is a simplified example. The cost per piece varies widely. This estimate does not include staff time. Non-profits generally offer members some type of service, like a publication, that costs money to produce and mail. On the other hand, non-profits ask for money more than once a year. Figuring that "the more you ask, the more you get," some organizations send an appeal for money with every piece of mail that goes out.

Businesses also prospect for customers. A catalog,

**Amount of direct mail
per age/income/education**

. . . as income, age, and education go up, so does the amount of direct mail.

| 0 | *Not much* | *Lots* | *Too much* |

however, can cost considerably more to produce and mail. According to Paul Hawken of Smith & Hawken, an average of 20 percent of the cost of a mail-order product goes toward name rental, paper, printing, and postage; the number can vary from 10 percent to 50 percent of the purchase price.

Businesses and charities target people who are most likely to respond to their solicitations. If you buy gardening supplies from one company, you are likely to get catalogs from other gardening supply companies. If you give to one environmental organization, you are likely to get requests from others. But it's not always so straightforward. In some states, for example, lists are available through the motor vehicles department. You may get a request from a charity simply because you own a Volvo or Saab, the assumption being that if you own a more expensive car, you can afford to make a donation.

It is no surprise that as income, age, and education go up, so does the amount of direct mail. Other factors—number of credit cards, number of adults and wage earners in a household, and number of financial accounts and

Over half of the adult population shops by mail.

Advertising mail...

Income	1st-class ads and stuffers	3rd-class mail from business	3rd-class mail from non-profit charities	Pieces/ wk	Total pieces of advt./ year
$10-14,900	1.4	6.0	1.6	9.0	468
$15-19,900	1.4	6.3	1.8	9.5	494
$20-24,900	1.8	7.4	1.8	11.0	572
$25-29,900	1.8	7.8	3.6	13.2	686
$30-34,900	2.5	8.8	2.5	13.8	718
$35-49,900	2.6	9.8	2.5	14.9	775
$50-64,900	3.3	11.7	2.9	17.9	931
$65-79,900	3.8	12.0	3.0	18.8	978
$80-99,900	3.5	14.5	4.0	22.0	1144
$100,000+	4.9	12.3	3.7	20.9	1087

The Environmental
Defense Fund
estimates that
households receive
an average of 84
pounds of third-class
mail per year . . .

insurance policies—are also closely tied to advertising mail. Previous buying or donating habits, of course, are key considerations.

According to the Postal Service's Household Diary Study for 1988, the most recent study available, households earning over $65,000 receive almost twice as many pieces of advertising mail (including requests from non-profits) as households that earn less than $20,000.

Not all of these pieces are junk mail (remember, junk mail is *unsolicited* and *unwanted*). Many people welcome the catalogs, newsletters from non-profits, and advertising flyers sent third class. Although over 33 percent of the respondents in the Postal Service's study said they wished they received less advertising mail, they did read or scan a substantial portion of what landed in their mailbox.

Participants said that, of their third-class mail, they read immediately and completely 41 to 49 percent of it, looked at 21 to 27 percent of it, put aside for future reading 8 percent of it, and discarded without reading 11 to 15 percent of it.

Shopping by mail is big business. According to the Direct Marketing Association, 98.6 million people—over 54 percent of the adult population—shopped by mail or by phone in 1990.

Environmental Problems

According to the U.S. Postal Service, over 63 billion pieces of third-class mail—including circulars, catalogs, advertisements, newsletters, and other printed matter—were mailed in fiscal year 1990. Many more billions of pieces of advertising were sent first class. An estimated 13.6 billion catalogs were mailed in 1990, over twice as many as were mailed 10 years ago.

These billions of pieces of paper come from trees. The trees are cut and trucked to mills, where they are pulped. The paper-making process uses copious quantities of water, chemicals, and energy. The process produces copious amounts of pollution in air, rivers and lakes. For example, dioxin—a highly toxic chemical—is created as a by-product when pulp is bleached with chlorine. Some inks used in printing contain toxic heavy metals.

Eventually, all direct mail, read or unread, must be taken to a landfill or incinerator, where it can contribute to groundwater contamination or air pollution. The Environmental Defense Fund, a national environmental organization, estimates that third-class mail makes up 2.5 percent of the waste from towns and cities across this country.

The watchwords for garbage in the 1990s are reduce, reuse, and recycle. That is, we must reduce the amount of waste we generate (in this case, curtailing duplicate catalogs and unwanted direct mail), reuse goods (saving a catalog for reference throughout the year), and recycle what cannot be reused.

Direct mail, however, is difficult to recycle and has low value. It often contains stickers, foil, adhesive, plastic, and decals which can contaminate the paper recycling process—so paper brokers and mills don't want it. To be recycled, direct mail must be taken apart by hand and sorted into categories (such as white paper, colored paper, coated paper, and non-recyclable material) set up by your town or city recycling program—if your town or city has such a program, and many don't. In programs which are just getting started, the emphasis is on high-value paper, not junk mail.

How many trees must be cut to support this country's direct mail habit? The figures are, at best, approximations. Conservatree Paper Company, a recycled-paper wholesaler, estimates that recycling a ton of paper saves 17 trees. The U.S. Postal Service reports that in 1988,

... but over 12 pounds per household is discarded without being read.

3.8 million tons of mail were shipped third class. At 17 trees per ton, 3.8 million tons of paper would require over 64 million trees.

The Postal Service's study shows that 11 to 15 percent of third-class mail delivered to households is discarded unread. Thus, each year an estimated 9 million trees are cut and manufactured into the ultimate junk mail—mail that is never even read.

Strategies for Stopping Junk Mail

So how do you stop junk mail? *The main goal is to put limits on the use of your name so that fewer people will be trading and renting it.* If you're not on the list, you won't get the catalog, advertising flyer, or solicitation letter.

You have two very effective tools at your disposal: your buying power and the considerable cost of doing business through direct mail. If you register with Mail Preference Service, withhold the use of your name whenever possible, patronize companies that will not give out your name, and make it very clear that certain solicitations are a waste of time and money, then you will make significant progress in the battle against junk mail.

Mail Preference Service

The Direct Marketing Association is a trade association representing more than 3,500 organizations and businesses. Members include publishers, catalog firms, list brokers, advertising agencies, insurance companies, non-profit organizations, fund raisers, and other groups that engage in direct marketing.

DMA offers Mail Preference Service to the public at no charge. If you register, your name will be removed from the lists sent to subscribers for five years. Since 80 percent of the national direct mail firms—including for-profit giants like L.L. Bean and Lands' End and non-profits like the National Wildlife Federation and The Nature

Conservancy—subscribe to Mail Preference Service, registering is an effective method of cutting down on national direct mail. The service will not, however, affect mail from local, state, or regional fund-raisers or businesses.

To register, use Card A. Send your name and address, plus all the variations under which you and members of your household receive mail. (DMA will not accept telephone registrations.) Then be patient. The service sends an update each January, April, July, and October to participating members, so you may not see results immediately. You may want to keep a list of the variations you send to DMA; if you're still getting a substantial amount of national direct mail six months later, check the addresses on those pieces to see if you're receiving them under another variation. If you are, write to DMA again.

Registering should reduce your national direct mail substantially.

While you're contacting the Direct Marketing Association, you can also register for Telephone Preference Service. The association will put your name and phone number on a list distributed to participating members so you will not receive unsolicited sales calls from them. The list of subscribers includes most major brokers of telephone lists.

DMA also sells the "Great Catalog Guide" for $3. The guide gives you the ability to survey 250 mail-order companies and choose ones that offer the merchandise and service you desire. The guide also notes whether the company will remove your name from its rental list.

If you are interested in ordering books by mail, for example, but you don't want your name rented, you can order from one of the companies in the catalog that will honor your request not to release your name.

Businesses that do not subscribe to Mail Preference Service

How can you decrease the flood of mail from the other 25 percent of the national advertising industry and from regional or local groups? First, you can use Cards C and E to contact mail-order companies, magazines, and newspapers with which you want to do business and tell them not to rent your name. And second, you can use Card G to write to businesses that solicit you and ask to be put on their suppression list, so that your name will be withheld from future prospecting mailings.

Remember that you are the customer and the customer is always right. If a business is not willing to agree to your terms, you can take your money elsewhere. Buying power is real power, especially when not just one person but thousands of people are stating their intentions.

Send the cards provided in this book. Or add a handwritten P.S. when you order by mail. Or use a check-off box if it's provided. Or call on a company's toll-free customer service line to make your request. In short, be consistent and be aggressive.

Your bank, credit card company, etc.

Take every opportunity to withhold use of your name. Mail Card F to any business that sends you a bill (utilities, department stores, credit card companies) or an account statement (banks, insurance companies, financial companies). If the company's consumer services department is at a different address than the billing department, send the postcard separately rather than including it with your payment. If you must send a confidential account number, like your credit card number, be sure to enclose the card in an envelope.

Some businesses are already sending out notices to their customers giving them a choice. Use the cards they send and add a P.S. saying "Thanks for asking!" to reinforce the policy.

Charities and membership organizations

You can get off the trade/rent lists of charities and organizations the same way that you get off other lists—by asking. Use card D. You can also request fewer solicitations from the organizations to which you belong. If you do your giving at the end of the year, for example, and won't respond to requests (no matter how urgent) at other times, then tell the membership department your preference.

Non-profits and associations may have lofty goals, but they operate like businesses, and they have a big stake in holding on to their members—in this case, you. They should be willing, if not eager, to accommodate your wishes.

Non-profits that are committed to conserving resources and curtailing wasteful mail can, like businesses, set up an in-house suppression list, provide members with a simple check-off to have their name withheld from being rented or traded, and send mailings to smaller, better targeted audiences.

The U. S. Postal Service

The U.S. Postal Service gives reduced rates to businesses and organizations that prepare mail so it's easy to handle. Options include using bar codes, using nine-digit ZIP codes, bundling all the pieces that go to one post office, and bundling all the pieces that go to specific carrier routes.

But bulk mail does not pay for itself. Although the Postal Rate Commission attempted to curtail the trend of first-class mail paying a disproportionate share of costs, when the commission recommended a rate schedule in January of 1991 the schedule still had first-class mail paying 124 percent and third-class mail 93 percent of the respective costs of delivery. In other words, the postage you pay on first-class mail helps cover the cost of delivering third-class mail.

CAR-RT SORT on the mailing label means that mail has been pre-sorted by the carrier route.

In the eyes of the Postal Service, the "customers" are mail-order companies, magazines, and non-profits—not you. And, as you remember, it is the customer who counts. Third-class mail makes up 39 percent of the volume handled by the Postal Service, and the service is unlikely to do anything that substantially limits its income.

However, the Postal Service does provide you—the consumer—with some options. If the direct mail piece carries the inscription "Address Correction Requested" or "Return Postage Guaranteed," don't open the envelope. Instead, write "Refused—Return to Sender" and the company will have to pay for the return postage.

If there is no inscription, open the envelope and see if there is a postage-paid envelope enclosed. If there is, stuff the promotional material into it and send it back to the organization—on the organization's tab.

If all else fails, you can simply refuse to accept the mail, using Card B. Postal regulations, presented in the "Conditions of Delivery" section of the *Domestic Mail Manual* (Issue 36, September 16, 1990) give you this option:

> The addressee may refuse to accept a piece of mail at the time it is offered for delivery...After delivery, an addressee may mark a piece of mail "Refused" and return it, unopened [except for registered, insured, certified, COD, and other special types of mail].

The Postal Service will simply toss this mail into the dead letter bin. From there, it will go to the landfill or incinerator. This method, then, is the least effective way of promoting change: the company or organization involved never receives the message. Your action does serve as a protest, however, and perhaps in the long run the Postal Service will respond to costs associated with hauling the returned mail back to the local post office and trucking it to the landfill.

Six Steps to Decreasing Junk Mail

1. *National advertising:* Register with the Direct Marketing Association to decrease by 75 percent the amount of national direct mail you receive.

2. *In-house mailing lists:* If you are a member of an organization, if you have bought merchandise from a company, or if someone has given you a mail-order gift, then you are on an in-house list. Contact these companies and tell them to remove your name from their in-house list (if you don't want to get material from them anymore) or to remove your name from the list that they rent or trade (if you want their material but not solicitations from other groups).

For the biggest return, first contact national companies and organizations, which would be most likely to give out your name most often; then contact regional, state, and local businesses and groups.

You can use the postcards provided in this book, add a note or use a check-off box on an order form, or tell the customer service representative directly if the company has a toll-free telephone number.

3. *Catalogs:* A growing number of companies will let you specify how many catalogs you want per year. As you contact each company to place an order or register for the no-rent designation, set a limit. Then, save the catalogs you do receive for future reference. If you are getting duplicates, send both labels and request that the extra copy be eliminated.

4. *Rented mailing lists:* Steps #1 and #2 should greatly cut down on the amount of direct mail you receive. If you get mail from a company or organization with which you do not do business, that group has probably rented or traded for your name. Use the postcards (or their toll-free numbers) to ask these groups to put you on their suppression list.

5. *More national advertising:* If, after six months, you are still getting national mail you don't want, determine whether the solicitations are arriving with a name and address that you did not send to Direct Marketing Association. If so, send another card with the new information.

6. Give out your name and address only when it is absolutely necessary, and then request that it not be given to anyone else.

Whenever possible, send the mailing label (which has the version of your name and address used by that particular business) with your request.

The Greening of Direct Mail

Many businesses are already developing "green" policies. Over half of the companies listed in the Direct Marketing Association's "Great Catalog Guide" offer name removal to their customers, ensuring that those names will not be rented to other businesses. In 1989, DMA itself set up a Task Force on Environmental Issues, a move which shows that the industry is sensitive to public opinion and the economics of "mailing smart."

Individual companies have already taken steps to limit wasteful mailing. For example, W.M. Green & Company, which markets gifts and home accessories, uses a box on the order form to secure information to streamline mailing. The form has check-offs so that customers can indicate whether their address is correct (so that mail will be delivered properly), whether they are getting duplicate catalogs, and whether they want to register for either the no-rent list or the suppression list.

Instead of sending out a new catalog in 1991, the Necessary Trading Company (which sells environmentally responsible products for home and garden) sent customers a postcard informing them that they could order products from the previous catalog—at 1990 prices. Customers who hadn't saved their catalog could return the postcard and get a replacement.

Seventh Generation, which sells conservation-oriented and environmentally-sensitive products, includes an order form—rather than a catalog—with each purchase. (In the terms of the trade, Seventh Generation uses a non-catalog "bounceback.") The company, like several others, promotes Mail Preference Service, allows customers to specify how many catalogs per year they want, and keeps a suppression list.

Smith & Hawken, which sells high quality tools, furniture, and clothing, issued a full-scale environmental policy in 1990 in which it pledged to: put a no trade/no rent check-off box on its order form and make the same offer to telephone customers; set up a suppression list; give a $5 gift certificate when customers return labels from duplicate catalogs; use recycled paper in its catalogs; use vegetable-based inks; give customers a choice of which catalogs they receive; and plant two trees for every tree it uses in catalog production.

Roberta Fortune's Almanac, which sells an eclectic mix of home, health, children's, and gift items, verifies addresses regularly through the National Change of Address program, has an active in-house mail preference service, and has strict data entry standards.

Rather than sending an entire catalog to the people on a rented list, Cabela's, a hunting and fishing goods company, has used two attached postcards. One card describes the company's merchandise and the other is a catalog request form.

Curtailing junk mail saves trees.

Companies are taking other steps to cut down on solid waste. Mountain Tools and Seventh Generation reuse boxes; Seventh Generation also uses boxes made of recycled fiber. Mountain Tools uses newspaper instead of "plastic peanuts" for packing material. ("Read up on local gossip and events!" the catalog says.) The Metropolitan Museum of Art no longer mails its catalogs in plastic bags. Patagonia, MacConnection, Seventh Generation, Esprit de Corp., Recreational Equipment, Inc., and other companies print their catalogs on paper with recycled content.

As you contact companies and non-profit organizations to urge them to "mail smart," you also have the opportunity to encourage "green" policies. The postcards in this book include some of these options, such as:

❖ encouraging the company to use a check-off so that people can easily register for the no trade/no rent or suppression status;

- ❖ telling the company that you are receiving duplicate mailings or more catalogs per year than you want;

- ❖ encouraging the company to use non-catalog bouncebacks;

- ❖ requesting the use of recycled paper and packaging;

- ❖ asking for "open" windows in envelopes or windows made from glassine (a thin, transparent paper) rather than plastic; and

- ❖ requesting that magazines discontinue the use of wrappers, especially plastic bags.

Of course, you can also add your own special suggestions and requests.

It costs a lot of money to print and mail catalogs. Mail-order companies must minimize the expense of prospecting for new customers while working to expand their customer list. Encouraging customers to report duplicate mailings and allowing them to specify how many catalogs they want annually make economic sense.

A Final Note

Keep a list so you'll know where you've sent cards. If your requests aren't honored, you can vote with your pen when it comes time to renew a subscription, rejoin an organization, make a donation, or buy merchandise.

Also remember that the cards will not banish junk mail from your life. Whenever you give people your name and address, you are giving them the opportunity to use, rent, or trade that information. While the cards can be very effective, you must be ever vigilant. It may be "company policy" to collect names and addresses when you purchase an item at a store, but if pushed the company may decide that your current purchase is more important than having your name on its list. In short, give your name and address only when it is absolutely necessary, and then request that they not be given to anyone else.

The information on the cards is included on the following pages so that if you use up all of the cards, you will have sample texts for writing postcards of your own. Or, you can order a Postcard Refill Pack (see page 25).

Sample Card Texts

Card A:

Mail this card to Direct Marketing Association

❏ I'd like to register for Mail Preference Service. I'm including all of the variations on name and address that come to this household.

❏ I'd also like to register for Telephone Preference Service. My number is: (_____) _____ - _____ .

Mail to:

Mail Preference Service, Direct Marketing Association, PO Box 3861, New York, New York 10163-3861

Card B:

Give this card to your letter-carrier or local postmaster

I am refusing this mail (and may be refusing mail in the future) because I did not ask for it and I do not want it. I understand that I have the right to refuse mail under Section 153, "Conditions of Delivery," of the Domestic Mail Manual (Issue 36, 9/16/1990).

I protest the U.S. Postal Service's rate structure, which subsidizes and encourages the use of bulk mail. If bulk mail contributed its proportionate share toward postal costs, there would be an economic incentive for bulk mailers to target their mailings more carefully, maintain suppression lists, verify addresses, eliminate duplications, and use other strategies to "mail smart."

Please forward this card to the Postmaster General.

Sincerely,

If you wish, you can send this card directly to the Postmaster General.

Card C:

If you're on an in-house list at a mail-order company, send this card

❏ Remove my name from your trade/rental list.

❏ Just send me _____ catalogs a year.

❏ Remove my name from your mailing list.

❏ Delete the duplicate copy that you're sending me.

❏ Please use recycled paper for your catalog.

❏ Mail smart: Join Mail Preference Service, set up a suppression list, put "no trade/no rent" and "suppression" check-off boxes on your order form, eliminate duplicates, and use non-catalog bouncebacks.

Card D:

If you're a member of an organization, send this card

- ❏ Remove my name from your trade/rental list.
- ❏ Send a renewal notice one month before my renewal is due and—at the end of the year—send one request for money. Skip all the other requests, because I won't respond.
- ❏ Delete the duplicate material that you're sending me.
- ❏ Use recycled paper and leave the windows in envelopes open (or use recyclable glassine).
- ❏ Mail smart: Join Mail Preference Service, set up a suppression list, and put "no trade/no rent" and "suppression" check-off boxes on your membership form.

Card E:

If you subscribe to a magazine or newspaper, send this card

- ❏ Remove my name from your trade/rental list.
- ❏ Delete the duplicate publication that you're sending me.
- ❏ Use recycled paper and leave the windows in envelopes open or use recyclable glassine.
- ❏ Skip the wrapper. If you must use one, use paper rather than plastic.
- ❏ Mail smart: Join Mail Preference Service, set up a suppression list, and put "no trade/no rent" and "suppression" check-off boxes on your renewal form.

Card F:

Mail this card to your bank, credit card company, utility, etc.

Please do not give out my name and address!

- ❏ I do not give permission for you to trade or rent my name, address, or telephone number. Please code my name "Privacy," "No mailing lists" or "No telemarketing solicitations."

DO NOT PLACE CONFIDENTIAL ACCOUNT IDENTIFICATION INFORMATION ON A POSTCARD. MAIL CARD IN AN ENVELOPE INSTEAD.

Card G:

If you are not a member of an organization or have not bought merchandise from the company, mail this card

Do not solicit me any more! I will not buy your merchandise, enter your sweepstakes, join your organization, or donate to your cause.

❏ Please put my name on your suppression list.

❏ Please forward this card to the person or business that supplied you with my name.

❏ Mail smart: Join Mail Preference Service, set up a suppression list, put "no trade/no rent" and "suppression" check-off boxes on your membership or order form, eliminate duplicates, and use non-catalog bouncebacks.

Keeping Track

Variations on name and address sent to Mail Preference Service:

1. _____

_____

_____

2. _____

_____

_____

3. _____

_____

_____

4. _____

_____

_____

Keeping Track

Date Request Sent

A: Mail Preference Service   _____

B: Letter Carrier/Post Office   _____

C: Mail Order Companies   _____

    1. _____ _____

    2. _____ _____

    3. _____ _____

    4. _____ _____

    5. _____ _____

    6. _____ _____

    7. _____ _____

    8. _____ _____

D: Organizations

    1. _____ _____

    2. _____ _____

    3. _____ _____

    4. _____ _____

    5. _____ _____

    6. _____ _____

    7. _____ _____

    8. _____ _____

Continued on next page

Keeping Track

E: Magazines and newspapers

1. _____   _____
2. _____   _____
3. _____   _____
4. _____   _____

F: Businesses

1. _____   _____
2. _____   _____
3. _____   _____
4. _____   _____
5. _____   _____
6. _____   _____

G: General: Do not solicit!

1. _____   _____
2. _____   _____
3. _____   _____
4. _____   _____

Yes! I'd like to do more to stop junk mail.

Please send me:

Totals

___ Postcard Refill Packs
(32 cards per pack) at $5 each   ___

___ Copies of *The Stop Junk Mail Book* at $6.95 each   ___

___ Postage and handling*   ___

Maine residents add:
$.25 tax per Refill Pack and $.35 tax per book   ___

Total enclosed $ ___

* Postage and Handling

Postcard pack	Free
1-2 books	$1.50
3-5 books	$2.00
6-9 books	$2.50
10+ books	$3.50

Suggestions or comments for the next edition:

_____

_____

_____

_____

_____

_____

Send to:
Georgetown Press, RFD 2, Box 535, Augusta, ME 04330

Cut and Send to Georgetown Press

Card A: Mail This Card to Direct Marketing Association

❑ I'd like to register for Mail Preference Service. I'm
   including all of the variations on name and address that
   come to this household.

❑ I'd also like to register for Telephone Preference
   Service. My number is: (_____) _____- _____ .
   Area Code

Put mailing labels or print names and addresses below.

_____

_____

_____

_____

From *The Stop Junk Mail Book.* Copyright © 1991 by Dorcas S. Miller

Card B: Give this card to your letter-carrier or local postmaster

I am refusing this mail (and may be refusing mail in the future) because I did not ask for it and I do not want it. I understand that I have the right to refuse mail under Section 153, "Conditions of Delivery," of the Domestic Mail Manual (Issue 36, 9/16/1990).

I protest the U.S. Postal Service's rate structure, which subsidizes and encourages the use of bulk mail. If bulk mail contributed its proportionate share toward postal costs, there would be an economic incentive for bulk mailers to target their mailings more carefully, maintain suppression lists, verify addresses, eliminate duplications, and use other strategies to "mail smart."

Please forward this card to the Postmaster General.

Sincerely,

From: _____

_____

_____

_____

Mail Preference Service
Direct Marketing Association
PO Box 3861
New York, New York 10163-3861

✂ —

From: _____

_____

_____

_____

Postmaster General
U.S. Postal Service
Washington, D.C. 20260

Card C: If you're on an in-house list at a mail-order company, send this card

❏ Remove my name from your trade/rental list.
❏ Just send me _____ catalogs a year.
❏ Remove my name from your mailing list.
❏ Delete the duplicate copy that you're sending me.*
❏ Please use recycled paper for your catalog.
❏ Mail smart: Join Mail Preference Service, set up a suppression list, put "no trade/no rent" and "suppression" check-off boxes on your order form, eliminate duplicates, and use non-catalog bouncebacks.

Put mailing label or print name and address here:

*Place duplicate label here

From *The Stop Junk Mail Book.* Copyright © 1991 by Dorcas S. Miller

✂ –

Card C: If you're on an in-house list at a mail-order company, send this card

❏ Remove my name from your trade/rental list.
❏ Just send me _____ catalogs a year.
❏ Remove my name from your mailing list.
❏ Delete the duplicate copy that you're sending me.*
❏ Please use recycled paper for your catalog.
❏ Mail smart: Join Mail Preference Service, set up a suppression list, put "no trade/no rent" and "suppression" check-off boxes on your order form, eliminate duplicates, and use non-catalog bouncebacks.

Put mailing label or print name and address here:

*Place duplicate label here

From *The Stop Junk Mail Book.* Copyright © 1991 by Dorcas S. Miller

From: _____

_____

_____

_____

Place
Postage
Stamp
Here

To: _____

_____

_____

_____

✂ —

From: _____

_____

_____

_____

Place
Postage
Stamp
Here

To: _____

_____

_____

_____

Card C: If you're on an in-house list at a mail-order company, send this card

❏ Remove my name from your trade/rental list.
❏ Just send me_____ catalogs a year.
❏ Remove my name from your mailing list.
❏ Delete the duplicate copy that you're sending me.*
❏ Please use recycled paper for your catalog.
❏ Mail smart: Join Mail Preference Service, set up a suppression list, put "no trade/no rent" and "suppression" check-off boxes on your order form, eliminate duplicates, and use non-catalog bouncebacks.

Put mailing label or print name and address here:

*Place duplicate label here

From *The Stop Junk Mail Book.* Copyright © 1991 by Dorcas S. Miller

✂ —

Card C: If you're on an in-house list at a mail-order company, send this card

❏ Remove my name from your trade/rental list.
❏ Just send me_____ catalogs a year.
❏ Remove my name from your mailing list.
❏ Delete the duplicate copy that you're sending me.*
❏ Please use recycled paper for your catalog.
❏ Mail smart: Join Mail Preference Service, set up a suppression list, put "no trade/no rent" and "suppression" check-off boxes on your order form, eliminate duplicates, and use non-catalog bouncebacks.

Put mailing label or print name and address here:

*Place duplicate label here

From *The Stop Junk Mail Book.* Copyright © 1991 by Dorcas S. Miller

From: _____
_____
_____
_____

To: _____
_____
_____
_____

✂ —

From: _____
_____
_____
_____

To: _____
_____
_____
_____

Card C: If you're on an in-house list at a mail-order company, send this card

❏ Remove my name from your trade/rental list.

❏ Just send me _____ catalogs a year.

❏ Remove my name from your mailing list.

❏ Delete the duplicate copy that you're sending me.*

❏ Please use recycled paper for your catalog.

❏ Mail smart: Join Mail Preference Service, set up a suppression list, put "no trade/no rent" and "suppression" check-off boxes on your order form, eliminate duplicates, and use non-catalog bouncebacks.

Put mailing label or print name and address here:

_____

_____

_____

*Place duplicate label here

From *The Stop Junk Mail Book.* Copyright © 1991 by Dorcas S. Miller

✂ —

Card C: If you're on an in-house list at a mail-order company, send this card

❏ Remove my name from your trade/rental list.

❏ Just send me _____ catalogs a year.

❏ Remove my name from your mailing list.

❏ Delete the duplicate copy that you're sending me.*

❏ Please use recycled paper for your catalog.

❏ Mail smart: Join Mail Preference Service, set up a suppression list, put "no trade/no rent" and "suppression" check-off boxes on your order form, eliminate duplicates, and use non-catalog bouncebacks.

Put mailing label or print name and address here:

_____

_____

_____

*Place duplicate label here

From *The Stop Junk Mail Book.* Copyright © 1991 by Dorcas S. Miller

From: _____

_____

_____

_____

To: _____

_____

_____

_____

✂ -- -- -- -- -- -- -- -- -- -- -- -- -- --

From: _____

_____

_____

_____

To: _____

_____

_____

_____

Card C: If you're on an in-house list at a mail-order company, send this card

❑ Remove my name from your trade/rental list.

❑ Just send me _____ catalogs a year.

❑ Remove my name from your mailing list.

❑ Delete the duplicate copy that you're sending me.*

❑ Please use recycled paper for your catalog.

❑ Mail smart: Join Mail Preference Service, set up a suppression list, put "no trade/no rent" and "suppression" check-off boxes on your order form, eliminate duplicates, and use non-catalog bouncebacks.

Put mailing label or print name and address here:

*Place duplicate label here

From *The Stop Junk Mail Book.* Copyright © 1991 by Dorcas S. Miller

✂ —

Card C: If you're on an in-house list at a mail-order company, send this card

❑ Remove my name from your trade/rental list.

❑ Just send me _____ catalogs a year.

❑ Remove my name from your mailing list.

❑ Delete the duplicate copy that you're sending me.*

❑ Please use recycled paper for your catalog.

❑ Mail smart: Join Mail Preference Service, set up a suppression list, put "no trade/no rent" and "suppression" check-off boxes on your order form, eliminate duplicates, and use non-catalog bouncebacks.

Put mailing label or print name and address here:

*Place duplicate label here

From *The Stop Junk Mail Book.* Copyright © 1991 by Dorcas S. Miller

From:

_____

_____

_____

To:

_____

_____

_____

✂ — — — — — — — — — — — — — — — —

From:

_____

_____

_____

To:

_____

_____

_____

Card D: If you're a member of an organization, send this card

❏ Remove my name from your trade/rental list.

❏ Send a renewal notice one month before my renewal is due and—at the end of the year—send one request for money. Skip all the other requests, because I won't respond.

❏ Delete the duplicate material that you're sending me.*

❏ Use recycled paper and leave the windows in envelopes open (or use recyclable glassine).

❏ Mail smart: Join Mail Preference Service, set up a suppression list, and put "no trade/no rent" and "suppression" check-off boxes on your membership form.

Put mailing label or print name and address here:

*Place duplicate label here

From *The Stop Junk Mail Book.* Copyright © 1991 by Dorcas S. Miller

✂ —

Card D: If you're a member of an organization, send this card

❏ Remove my name from your trade/rental list.

❏ Send a renewal notice one month before my renewal is due and—at the end of the year—send one request for money. Skip all the other requests, because I won't respond.

❏ Delete the duplicate material that you're sending me.*

❏ Use recycled paper and leave the windows in envelopes open (or use recyclable glassine).

❏ Mail smart: Join Mail Preference Service, set up a suppression list, and put "no trade/no rent" and "suppression" check-off boxes on your membership form.

Put mailing label or print name and address here:

*Place duplicate label here

From *The Stop Junk Mail Book.* Copyright © 1991 by Dorcas S. Miller

From: _____

_____

_____

_____

To: _____

_____

_____

_____

✂ -

From: _____

_____

_____

_____

To: _____

_____

_____

_____

Card D: If you're a member of an organization, send this card

❏ Remove my name from your trade/rental list.

❏ Send a renewal notice one month before my renewal is due and—at the end of the year—send one request for money. Skip all the other requests, because I won't respond.

❏ Delete the duplicate material that you're sending me.*

❏ Use recycled paper and leave the windows in envelopes open (or use recyclable glassine).

❏ Mail smart: Join Mail Preference Service, set up a suppression list, and put "no trade/no rent" and "suppression" check-off boxes on your membership form.

Put mailing label or print name and address here:

_____

_____

_____

*Place duplicate label here

From *The Stop Junk Mail Book.* Copyright © 1991 by Dorcas S. Miller

✂ -

Card D: If you're a member of an organization, send this card

❏ Remove my name from your trade/rental list.

❏ Send a renewal notice one month before my renewal is due and—at the end of the year—send one request for money. Skip all the other requests, because I won't respond.

❏ Delete the duplicate material that you're sending me.*

❏ Use recycled paper and leave the windows in envelopes open (or use recyclable glassine).

❏ Mail smart: Join Mail Preference Service, set up a suppression list, and put "no trade/no rent" and "suppression" check-off boxes on your membership form.

Put mailing label or print name and address here:

_____

_____

_____

*Place duplicate label here

From *The Stop Junk Mail Book.* Copyright © 1991 by Dorcas S. Miller

From: _____

_____

_____

_____

To: _____

_____

_____

_____

✂ –

From: _____

_____

_____

_____

To: _____

_____

_____

_____

Card D: If you're a member of an organization, send this card

❏ Remove my name from your trade/rental list.

❏ Send a renewal notice one month before my renewal is due and—at the end of the year—send one request for money. Skip all the other requests, because I won't respond.

❏ Delete the duplicate material that you're sending me.*

❏ Use recycled paper and leave the windows in envelopes open (or use recyclable glassine).

❏ Mail smart: Join Mail Preference Service, set up a suppression list, and put "no trade/no rent" and "suppression" check-off boxes on your membership form.

Put mailing label or print name and address here:

*Place duplicate label here

From *The Stop Junk Mail Book.* Copyright © 1991 by Dorcas S. Miller

✄ —

Card D: If you're a member of an organization, send this card

❏ Remove my name from your trade/rental list.

❏ Send a renewal notice one month before my renewal is due and—at the end of the year—send one request for money. Skip all the other requests, because I won't respond.

❏ Delete the duplicate material that you're sending me.*

❏ Use recycled paper and leave the windows in envelopes open (or use recyclable glassine).

❏ Mail smart: Join Mail Preference Service, set up a suppression list, and put "no trade/no rent" and "suppression" check-off boxes on your membership form.

Put mailing label or print name and address here:

*Place duplicate label here

From *The Stop Junk Mail Book.* Copyright © 1991 by Dorcas S. Miller

From:

_____

_____

_____

_____

To:

_____

_____

_____

_____

✂ –

From:

_____

_____

_____

_____

To:

_____

_____

_____

_____

Card D: If you're a member of an organization, send this card

❏ Remove my name from your trade/rental list.

❏ Send a renewal notice one month before my renewal is due and—at the end of the year—send one request for money. Skip all the other requests, because I won't respond.

❏ Delete the duplicate material that you're sending me.*

❏ Use recycled paper and leave the windows in envelopes open (or use recyclable glassine).

❏ Mail smart: Join Mail Preference Service, set up a suppression list, and put "no trade/no rent" and "suppression" check-off boxes on your membership form.

Put mailing label or print name and address here:

*Place duplicate label here

From *The Stop Junk Mail Book*. Copyright © 1991 by Dorcas S. Miller

---

Card D: If you're a member of an organization, send this card

❏ Remove my name from your trade/rental list.

❏ Send a renewal notice one month before my renewal is due and—at the end of the year—send one request for money. Skip all the other requests, because I won't respond.

❏ Delete the duplicate material that you're sending me.*

❏ Use recycled paper and leave the windows in envelopes open (or use recyclable glassine).

❏ Mail smart: Join Mail Preference Service, set up a suppression list, and put "no trade/no rent" and "suppression" check-off boxes on your membership form.

Put mailing label or print name and address here:

*Place duplicate label here

From *The Stop Junk Mail Book*. Copyright © 1991 by Dorcas S. Miller

From: _____

_____

_____

_____

To: _____

_____

_____

_____

✂ —

From: _____

_____

_____

_____

To: _____

_____

_____

_____

Card E: If you subscribe to a magazine or newspaper, mail this card

❏ Remove my name from your trade/rental list.

❏ Delete the duplicate publication that you're sending me.*

❏ Use recycled paper and leave the windows in envelopes open or use recyclable glassine.

❏ Skip the wrapper. If you must use one, use paper rather than plastic.

❏ Mail smart: Join Mail Preference Service, set up a suppression list, and put "no trade/no rent" and "suppression" check-off boxes on your renewal form.

Put mailing label or print name and address here:

*Place duplicate label here

From *The Stop Junk Mail Book.* Copyright © 1991 by Dorcas S. Miller

✂ —

Card E: If you subscribe to a magazine or newspaper, mail this card

❏ Remove my name from your trade/rental list.

❏ Delete the duplicate publication that you're sending me.*

❏ Use recycled paper and leave the windows in envelopes open or use recyclable glassine.

❏ Skip the wrapper. If you must use one, use paper rather than plastic.

❏ Mail smart: Join Mail Preference Service, set up a suppression list, and put "no trade/no rent" and "suppression" check-off boxes on your renewal form.

Put mailing label or print name and address here:

*Place duplicate label here

From *The Stop Junk Mail Book.* Copyright © 1991 by Dorcas S. Miller

From: _____

_____

_____

_____

Place
Postage
Stamp
Here

To: _____

_____

_____

_____

✂ —

From: _____

_____

_____

_____

Place
Postage
Stamp
Here

To: _____

_____

_____

_____

Card E: If you subscribe to a magazine or newspaper, mail this card

- ❏ Remove my name from your trade/rental list.
- ❏ Delete the duplicate publication that you're sending me.*
- ❏ Use recycled paper and leave the windows in envelopes open or use recyclable glassine.
- ❏ Skip the wrapper. If you must use one, use paper rather than plastic.
- ❏ Mail smart: Join Mail Preference Service, set up a suppression list, and put "no trade/no rent" and "suppression" check-off boxes on your renewal form.

Put mailing label or print name and address here:

*Place duplicate label here

From *The Stop Junk Mail Book*. Copyright © 1991 by Dorcas S. Miller

✂ —

Card E: If you subscribe to a magazine or newspaper, mail this card

- ❏ Remove my name from your trade/rental list.
- ❏ Delete the duplicate publication that you're sending me.*
- ❏ Use recycled paper and leave the windows in envelopes open or use recyclable glassine.
- ❏ Skip the wrapper. If you must use one, use paper rather than plastic.
- ❏ Mail smart: Join Mail Preference Service, set up a suppression list, and put "no trade/no rent" and "suppression" check-off boxes on your renewal form.

Put mailing label or print name and address here:

*Place duplicate label here

From *The Stop Junk Mail Book*. Copyright © 1991 by Dorcas S. Miller

From: _____

_____

_____

_____

To: _____

_____

_____

_____

✂ ─

From: _____

_____

_____

_____

To: _____

_____

_____

_____

Card F: Mail this card to your bank, credit card company, utility, etc.

Please do not give out my name and address!

❏ I do not give permission for you to trade or rent my name, address, or telephone number. Please code my name "Privacy," "No mailing lists" or "No telemarketing solicitations."

Do not place confidential account identification information on a post card. Mail card in an envelope instead.

Put mailing label or print name and address here:

From *The Stop Junk Mail Book.* Copyright © 1991 by Dorcas S. Miller

✂ —

Card F: Mail this card to your bank, credit card company, utility, etc.

Please do not give out my name and address!

❏ I do not give permission for you to trade or rent my name, address, or telephone number. Please code my name "Privacy," "No mailing lists" or "No telemarketing solicitations."

Do not place confidential account identification information on a post card. Mail card in an envelope instead.

Put mailing label or print name and address here:

From *The Stop Junk Mail Book.* Copyright © 1991 by Dorcas S. Miller

From: _____

_____

_____

_____

To: _____

_____

_____

_____

✂ –

From: _____

_____

_____

_____

To: _____

_____

_____

_____

Card F: Mail this card to your bank, credit card company, utility, etc.

Please do not give out my name and address!

❑ I do not give permission for you to trade or rent my name, address, or telephone number. Please code my name "Privacy," "No mailing lists" or "No telemarketing solicitations."

Do not place confidential account identification information on a post card. Mail card in an envelope instead.

Put mailing label or print name and address here:

_____

_____

_____

From *The Stop Junk Mail Book.* Copyright © 1991 by Dorcas S. Miller

✂ —

Card F: Mail this card to your bank, credit card company, utility, etc.

Please do not give out my name and address!

❑ I do not give permission for you to trade or rent my name, address, or telephone number. Please code my name "Privacy," "No mailing lists" or "No telemarketing solicitations."

Do not place confidential account identification information on a post card. Mail card in an envelope instead.

Put mailing label or print name and address here:

_____

_____

_____

From *The Stop Junk Mail Book.* Copyright © 1991 by Dorcas S. Miller

From: _____

_____

_____

_____

To: _____

_____

_____

_____

✂ –

From: _____

_____

_____

_____

To: _____

_____

_____

_____

Card F: Mail this card to your bank, credit card company, utility, etc.

Please do not give out my name and address!

❑ I do not give permission for you to trade or rent my name, address, or telephone number. Please code my name "Privacy," "No mailing lists" or "No telemarketing solicitations."

Do not place confidential account identification information on a post card. Mail card in an envelope instead.

Put mailing label or print name and address here:

From *The Stop Junk Mail Book.* Copyright © 1991 by Dorcas S. Miller

----

Card F: Mail this card to your bank, credit card company, utility, etc.

Please do not give out my name and address!

❑ I do not give permission for you to trade or rent my name, address, or telephone number. Please code my name "Privacy," "No mailing lists" or "No telemarketing solicitations."

Do not place confidential account identification information on a post card. Mail card in an envelope instead.

Put mailing label or print name and address here:

From *The Stop Junk Mail Book.* Copyright © 1991 by Dorcas S. Miller

From: _____

_____

_____

_____

To: _____

_____

_____

_____

✂ –

From: _____

_____

_____

_____

To: _____

_____

_____

_____

Card G: If you are not a member of an organization or have not bought merchandise from a company, mail this card

Do not solicit me any more! I will not buy your merchandise, enter your sweepstakes, join your organization, or donate to your cause.

❏ Please put my name on your suppression list.

❏ Please forward this card to the person or business that supplied you with my name.

❏ Mail smart: Join Mail Preference Service, set up a suppression list, put "no trade/no rent" and "suppression" check-off boxes on your membership or order form, eliminate duplicates, and use non-catalog bouncebacks.

Put mailing label or print name and address here:

From *The Stop Junk Mail Book*. Copyright © 1991 by Dorcas S. Miller

✂ —

Card G: If you are not a member of an organization or have not bought merchandise from a company, mail this card

Do not solicit me any more! I will not buy your merchandise, enter your sweepstakes, join your organization, or donate to your cause.

❏ Please put my name on your suppression list.

❏ Please forward this card to the person or business that supplied you with my name.

❏ Mail smart: Join Mail Preference Service, set up a suppression list, put "no trade/no rent" and "suppression" check-off boxes on your membership or order form, eliminate duplicates, and use non-catalog bouncebacks.

Put mailing label or print name and address here:

From *The Stop Junk Mail Book*. Copyright © 1991 by Dorcas S. Miller

From: _____

_____

_____

_____

Place
Postage
Stamp
Here

To: _____

_____

_____

_____

✂ –

From: _____

_____

_____

_____

Place
Postage
Stamp
Here

To: _____

_____

_____

_____

Card G: If you are not a member of an organization or have not bought merchandise from a company, mail this card

Do not solicit me any more! I will not buy your merchandise, enter your sweepstakes, join your organization, or donate to your cause.

❏ Please put my name on your suppression list.

❏ Please forward this card to the person or business that supplied you with my name.

❏ Mail smart: Join Mail Preference Service, set up a suppression list, put "no trade/no rent" and "suppression" check-off boxes on your membership or order form, eliminate duplicates, and use non-catalog bouncebacks.

Put mailing label or print name and address here:

From *The Stop Junk Mail Book.* Copyright © 1991 by Dorcas S. Miller

✂ —

Card G: If you are not a member of an organization or have not bought merchandise from a company, mail this card

Do not solicit me any more! I will not buy your merchandise, enter your sweepstakes, join your organization, or donate to your cause.

❏ Please put my name on your suppression list.

❏ Please forward this card to the person or business that supplied you with my name.

❏ Mail smart: Join Mail Preference Service, set up a suppression list, put "no trade/no rent" and "suppression" check-off boxes on your membership or order form, eliminate duplicates, and use non-catalog bouncebacks.

Put mailing label or print name and address here:

From *The Stop Junk Mail Book.* Copyright © 1991 by Dorcas S. Miller

From: _____

_____

_____

_____

To: _____

_____

_____

_____

✂ ┄┄┄

From: _____

_____

_____

_____

To: _____

_____

_____

_____